our Environment

Nuclear Power

Bonnie Juettner

KIDHAVEN PRESS
An imprint of Thomson Gale, a part of The Thomson Corporation

THOMSON
GALE

Detroit • New York • San Francisco • New Haven, Conn. • Waterville, Maine • London

© 2007 Thomson Gale, a part of The Thomson Corporation.

Thomson and Star Logo are trademarks and Gale and KidHaven Press are registered trademarks used herein under license.

For more information, contact
KidHaven Press
27500 Drake Rd.
Farmington Hills, MI 48331-3535
Or you can visit our Internet site at http://www.gale.com

ALL RIGHTS RESERVED.
No part of this work covered by the copyright hereon may be reproduced or used in any form or by any means—graphic, electronic, or mechanical, including photocopying, recording, taping, Web distribution or information storage retrieval systems—without the written permission of the publisher.

Every effort has been made to trace the owners of copyrighted material.

Picture Credits:
Cover: The Image Bank/Getty Images; Associated Press, AP, 16-17; © CORBIS, 14; © Igor Kostin/Sygma/CORBIS, 19; © Roger Ressmeyer/CORBIS, 31, 32; © Royalty free/CORBIS, 29, 38; © Tim Wright/CORBIS, 15; Santi Burgos/Bloomberg News/Landov, 9; Kyodo/Landov, 11, 22; Newhouse News Service/Landov, 21; Reuters/Reinhard Krause/Landov, 35, 40; Steve Zmina, 37

LIBRARY OF CONGRESS CATALOGING-IN-PUBLICATION DATA

Juettner, Bonnie.
  Nuclear power / by Bonnie Juettner.
    p. cm. — (Our environment)
  Includes bibliographical references.
  ISBN 13: 978-0-7377-3618-2 (hardcover : alk. paper)
  ISBN 10: 0-7377-3618-6 (hardcover : alk. paper)
  1. Nuclear energy—Juvenile literature. I. Title.
  QC792.5.J84 2007
  333.792'4—dc22
                                                    2006019162

Printed in the United States of America

contents

Chapter 1
What Is Nucear Power?   4

Chapter 2
Concerns About Nuclear Power   13

Chapter 3
The Promise of Nuclear Power   24

Chapter 4
The Future of Nuclear Power   33

Glossary   42

For Further Exploration   44

Index   46

About the Author   48

chapter one

What Is Nuclear Power?

All matter is made of atoms, tiny particles that are too small to see without a very powerful microscope. The center of an atom is called the **nucleus**. The forces that hold a nucleus together are very strong. When the nucleus of an atom splits, the energy of those nuclear forces is released. Splitting the nucleus of just one atom produces a huge amount of energy. When this energy is collected and put to use, it is called **nuclear power**.

Splitting the Atom

Nuclear power gets its name from the word *nucleus*. The nucleus of an atom contains almost all of

What Is Nuclear Power? 5

its mass, but only one-trillionth of its volume. It takes very strong forces to hold all the mass of an atom in such a small area. These forces, which are called **nuclear forces**, are so strong that atoms almost never split in nature. (Scientists know of just one case when a uranium atom did split on its own. They believe this happened about 2 billion years ago in Africa.)

Scientists have just begun to learn about nuclear forces, so they still do not fully understand them. They do know that nuclear forces get weaker when

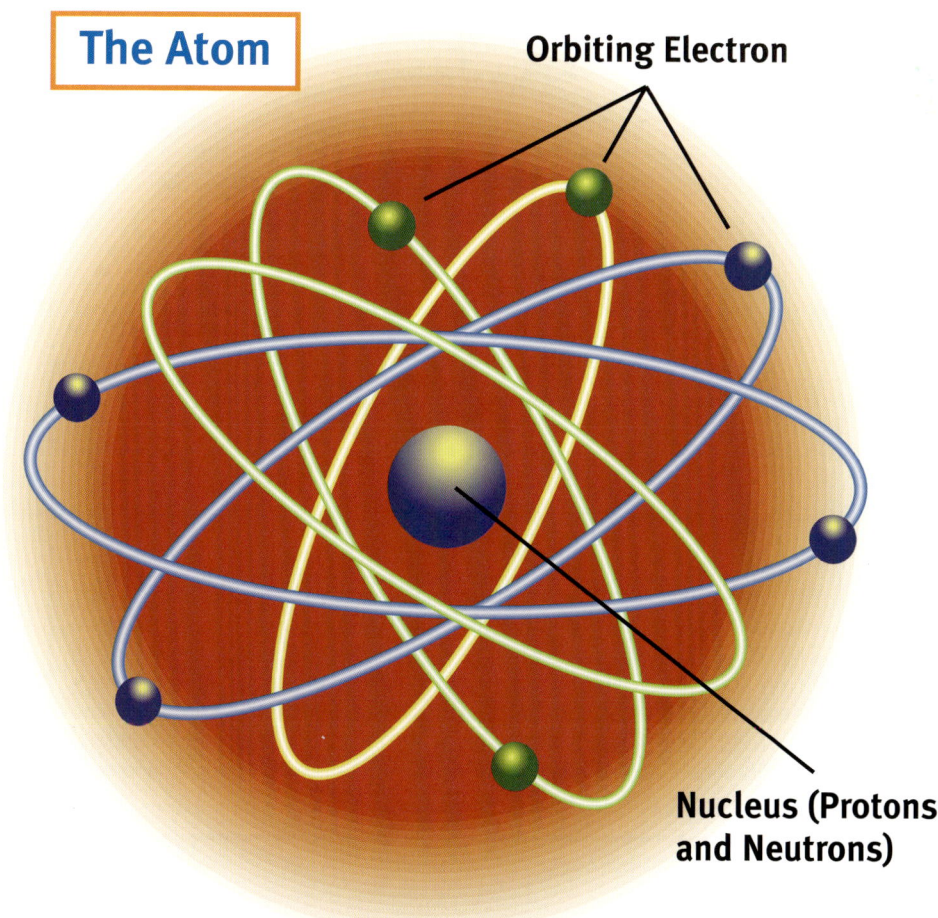

The Atom

Orbiting Electron

Nucleus (Protons and Neutrons)

6 Nuclear Power

they have to operate across longer distances. The smaller the nucleus of an atom, the stronger the nuclear force is. The larger the nucleus of the atom, the weaker the nuclear force is. Some atoms have very large nuclei, with more than 164 nucleons, small particles that make up the nucleus. In these atoms, the nuclear force is weaker along the edges

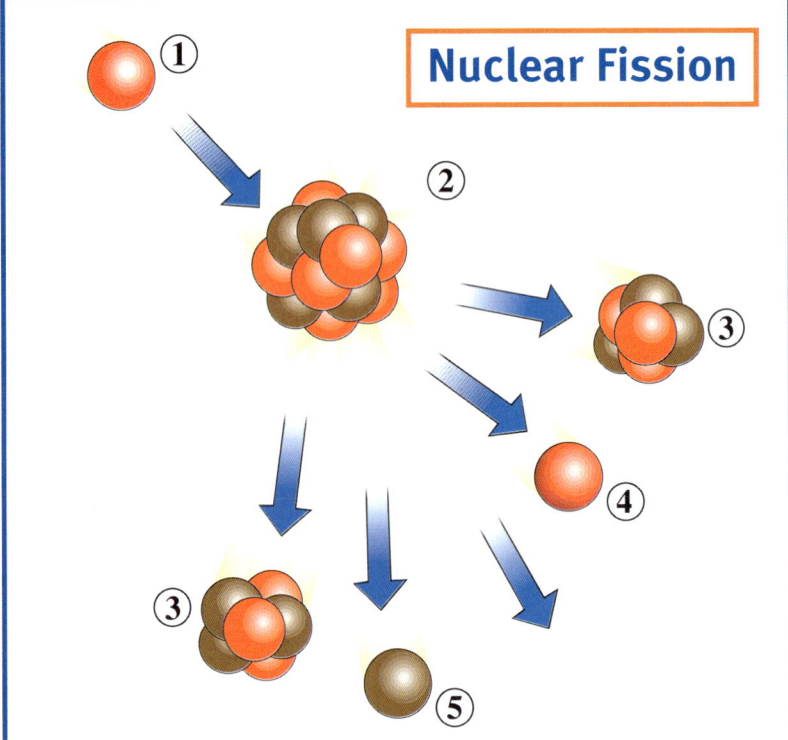

Nuclear Fission

Fission is the splitting of a heavy atom into two smaller parts. The energy created from the fission of an atom can be used to power nuclear reactors. The fission process begins when a tiny particle (1) is sent smashing into a heavy atom (2), breaking it apart into two smaller atoms (3). When the larger atom is split, it not only creates smaller atoms but also releases some extra electrons (4) and neutrons (5). At the same time, a tremendous amount of heat and radiation is released from the atom. This heat and radiation is used to provide energy.

of the nucleus, and the nucleus is a little bit unstable. On the other hand, atoms with smaller nuclei, such as atoms of the element carbon (the primary component of coal), have strong nuclear forces and are very stable. Carbon has only 12 nucleons.

Because nuclear forces are so strong, splitting the nucleus of an atom is a difficult feat. The process of splitting the nucleus of an atom is called **fission**. To do it, nuclear power plants use atoms from U-235, a rare form of the element **uranium**. This element has very large nuclei. The nuclei of U-235 contain 235 nucleons. Like other elements with such large nuclei, it is slightly unstable. To split a nucleus of U-235, scientists fire neutrons at a sample of uranium. A neutron is a kind of nuclear particle. A neutron hitting a nucleus of U-235 can push it from a circular shape into more of an elongated, oval shape. Once the nucleus lengthens past a critical point, it splits in two.

As fission occurs, a tremendous amount of energy, the equivalent of about 200 million electron volts, is released. (The explosion of one molecule of TNT releases 30 electron volts.) This energy can be harnessed and used to run an electric power plant. Atomic fission releases huge amounts of energy. It releases 10 million times the amount of energy produced by burning an atom of coal. This means that a small amount of uranium can be used to provide power for very long periods of time. For example, the fission of just one kilogram (2.2 lbs) of uranium in a nuclear power plant can provide power to a 100-watt lightbulb for 690 years.

Nuclear Power Worldwide

The technology used to harness nuclear power and make it into electricity is a little more than half a century old. Nuclear power is a relatively new form of energy. It is newer than coal- or oil-burning power plants or hydroelectric power plants. (Hydroelectric power plants harness the energy of moving water.) Most of the nuclear power plants currently operating in the United States and Western Europe were originally planned and ordered in the 1960s and 1970s. (Some, however, were not completed until much later. The newest nuclear power plant in the United States began operating in 1996.) The hydroelectric power plant at the Hoover Dam, by contrast, was built in the 1930s. The first coal-burning electric power plants in the United States were built in the late 1800s.

 Worldwide, most electric power plants still produce electricity by burning coal, not by splitting atoms of uranium. Some power plants harness the energy of wind or water. The amount of nuclear energy used by the United States and the rest of the world is growing, however. In 1971, when the nuclear energy industry was still young, nuclear energy provided 2.1 percent of the world's electricity. Since that time, the world's energy demands have increased dramatically. Currently, nuclear power provides almost 16 percent of the world's electricity. But that is still more than the total amount of electricity produced from all sources in 1960.

There are 440 nuclear power plants around the world, in 31 countries. Seventeen of those countries (including Japan, Germany, and Finland) rely on nuclear power for at least a quarter of their energy. Belgium, Bulgaria, Hungary, Slovakia, South Korea, Sweden, Switzerland, Slovenia, and Ukraine depend

This nuclear power plant in Guadalajara, Spain, is just one of many such plants around the world.

on nuclear power plants for one-third of their energy, or more. Some countries, such as France and Lithuania, rely on nuclear power for more than 70 percent of their energy. The United States has more nuclear power plants than any other country, but it gets only 20 percent of its total energy from nuclear power.

Nuclear-Powered Vehicles

Some countries, including Russia and the United States, also use nuclear power to provide energy for very large vehicles, such as aircraft carriers and submarines. Only a very large vehicle can be powered this way, because nuclear engines must be shielded by several feet of concrete—too much concrete to put into a car or truck. The concrete shields protect passengers from radiation. (Unstable elements, such as uranium, are radioactive. They radiate, or give off, alpha, beta, or gamma particles, which are dangerous for humans.) It takes about a pound (.5 kg) of uranium (a baseball-size amount) to power a submarine or aircraft carrier. Without nuclear engines, submarines and aircraft carriers would have to carry about a million gallons of gasoline. This amount would fill a cube the size of a five-story building.

The discovery of nuclear energy brought huge changes to the electric power industry. Before scientists could harness nuclear energy, though, they

The aircraft carrier USS Abraham Lincoln *enters a port in Japan. Nuclear energy powers America's aircraft carriers.*

had to figure out how to control a fission reaction. They also had to learn how to collect the energy that is released. They had to figure out how to protect people from accidents and how to prevent the radiation that is given off by uranium from being released into the community. Over the years, concerns about waste disposal and nuclear radiation have led people in many countries to debate the use of nuclear power.

chapter two

Concerns About Nuclear Power

The nuclear power industry is not expanding everywhere. In 1986 Italy shut down all its nuclear reactors. Germany's leaders have announced that they plan to gradually shut down all German reactors. Nuclear reactors currently produce one-third of Germany's electricity. No new nuclear power plants have been ordered in the United States since the 1970s. Why are so many people worried about nuclear power?

Radioactivity

Some elements have very large nuclei. These elements tend to be unstable. The nuclear forces that

A researcher holds a container of raw uranium, which will be used to make nuclear energy.

bind their nuclei together are weaker on the edges, and from time to time a particle escapes. Elements that lose particles this way are **radioactive**. Radioactivity is a type of **radiation**, energy that travels in particles or waves. Sunlight and heat are forms of radiation. So are radio waves, microwaves, and X-rays. People are exposed to low levels of radiation all the time. But high levels of radiation can cause people to become seriously ill or die. Exposure to radiation also can cause people to develop cancer years later.

Nuclear power plants use uranium, a mildly radioactive element, as fuel. They also produce highly

Concerns About Nuclear Power 15

radioactive **nuclear waste**. Uranium is relatively safe to handle *before* it has been used in a nuclear plant. (It is dangerous to ingest, if particles of it get into the air or water. This is not just because it is radioactive, but also because it is poisonous.) As atoms of uranium

A spent nuclear fuel rod containing radioactive waste glows an eerie blue in a cooling pond.

split, though, they form other elements that are much more radioactive. Radioactivity is measured in rems. The nuclear waste from an entire reactor gives off about 10,000 rems per hour, even ten years after it was first used in a nuclear plant. A human who is exposed to 500 rems at one time will die.

If nuclear waste were to leak into groundwater or rivers, it might enter food chains. The amount of radioactivity people could be exposed to through the food supply is small. It is far less than the dose that would be produced by exposure to an entire reactor's worth of waste. It would be diluted, not concentrated in one place. But it could still hurt people and animals when they ingest it. It would kill cells in the digestive tract, for example. And it could cause cancer to develop years later.

Storing Nuclear Waste

The elements that make up nuclear waste are unstable. Given time, they will decay enough that they will no longer be radioactive. However, it takes tens of thousands of years for nuclear waste to decay

Crew members work at Yucca Mountain in Nevada, where spent nuclear waste and other radioactive materials may one day be stored.

enough to be safe for humans. During that time, nuclear waste must be stored.

The problem of what to do with nuclear waste is controversial. One option is to reprocess it, because then much of it can be recycled. Japan ships its nuclear waste overseas for reprocessing. The United States does not currently reprocess nuclear waste. Many people in the United States fear that an accident could occur while the waste is being transported to a reprocessing facility. The U.S. also has no permanent storage facility for nuclear waste.

The nuclear industry in the United States hopes to bury its waste deep underground at Yucca Mountain, Nevada. But Nevadans have protested that they do not want nuclear waste in their state. Residents of other states have also protested. They do not want nuclear waste transported through their states. Currently, nuclear waste in the United States is stored in cooling pools of water and in dry storage casks at nuclear power plants.

Even if a solution can be found to the problem of nuclear waste, antinuclear activists say, nuclear power would still not be safe enough. They worry about what might happen if an accident occurs at a nuclear power plant.

The Chernobyl Accident

In 1986, the worst accident in the history of the nuclear power industry occurred. It happened at the Chernobyl plant in Ukraine. Worker mistakes caused several explosions. The explosions caused a fireball and blew the roof off a reactor. A cloud of radioactive dust was thrown into the air, and wind carried the cloud across Scandinavia, Eastern Europe, Canada, and parts of the United States.

The accident put 500 times more radioactivity into the atmosphere than was caused by the atom-

Concerns About Nuclear Power

ic bomb dropped on the city of Hiroshima, Japan, during World War II. In the accident itself, 32 people died. Many more became sick and died in the years that followed.

Safety Precautions

The Chernobyl plant was poorly designed. But engineers learned from what happened there and have made important changes to reactor designs. First, the Chernobyl reactor did not have a containment

The ruins of the Chernobyl nuclear power plant in Ukraine are a stark reminder of the 1986 accident that took place there.

structure to trap escaping radiation in the reactor building. Modern reactors are surrounded by a 5-inch-thick steel wall (12.7cm) and a 3- to 6-foot-thick concrete barrier (.9 to 1.8m).

Second, nuclear reactors are designed to slow down the fission process. When one atom of uranium splits, it sends off two or three neutrons. These neutrons hit other atoms of uranium and cause more fissions. This process is called a **chain reaction**. If it gets out of control, it can cause an explosion. So nuclear reactors separate lumps of uranium with a material that slows down, but does not stop, escaping neutrons. Modern reactors use water, which cannot catch fire, to slow down neutrons. Older reactors, like Chernobyl, used graphite, which catches fire if it gets hot enough.

Third, reactors today are designed to stop operators from making foolish mistakes. For example, nuclear reactors have control rods made of a metal that can absorb and stop neutrons. If a chain reaction is getting out of control, the control rods are inserted into the reactor to stop the reaction. At Chernobyl, electrical engineers conducting an experiment had withdrawn 205 control rods, leaving only 6. To accomplish this, they disconnected the reactor's safety systems. Today, though, every feature of a reactor now has two or more safety systems. If one system stops operating, the other will remain in place.

Leaking acid ate through this steel lid covering a nuclear reactor core in Ohio in 2002.

Recent Accidents

Regular inspections at nuclear plants have prevented some accidents. In 2002, workers at an Ohio plant discovered that the 6.5-inch-thick steel lid (16.5cm) on top of the reactor's core had corroded away. They found less than half an inch (1.3cm) of steel between the reactor and the containment building. The reactor was immediately shut down for repairs. In 2003 a worker lost a 1-inch screw (2.5cm) during refueling of the nuclear power plant in Zorita, Spain. The reactor was instantly shut down while employees searched for the screw.

22 Nuclear Power

In spite of design changes and rigorous safety regulations, though, accidents at nuclear power plants still happen. In 2005 pipes broke at a nuclear fuel reprocessing plant in Britain, and fuel leaked into the plant. In 2006 several U.S. nuclear reactors were found to be leaking radioactive water into the ground. (However, the water was only mildly radioactive. The water was similar to the water reactors are legally permitted to release into public waterways.)

Four workers died at a Japanese nuclear facility when this broken pipe allowed superhot water and steam to escape.

The worst accidents in recent years have occurred in Japan, which has the third-largest nuclear industry in the world. There have been fires and water leaks. In 1999 worker mistakes led to a chain reaction at Tokaimura. Fifty-five workers were exposed to 15,000 times more radiation than usual. In 2004 a pipe at the Mihama plant broke. Boiling water and steam burst out, killing five people and injuring six others. The plant was closed, but in 2006 it began to leak radioactive water inside its containment building.

Despite the risks, nuclear advocates argue that nuclear power is much safer for people and the environment than fossil fuel–based energy systems. Nuclear power, they say, will be the clean energy of the future.

chapter three

The Promise of Nuclear Power

In the early years of nuclear energy, most environmentalists were opposed to it. They feared the damage to the environment that could result from an accident. They also suspected that it was not possible to safeguard nuclear waste for tens of thousands of years. In recent years, though, many environmentalists have changed their minds. Why do they consider nuclear power to be a "clean" energy source? They have compared it with the energy source that provides most of the world's energy: fossil fuels.

Fossil Fuels and the Environment

Many environmentalists now feel that nuclear power plants should not be expected to be perfect.

It is enough, they say, to expect nuclear power to be safer and better for the environment than coal-burning power plants.

In the United States, there are more than 600 coal-burning power plants producing 60 percent of the country's electricity. These plants release toxic chemicals into the air, causing air pollution. They release 64 percent of all the sulfur dioxide that is given off in the United States, 26 percent of nitrogen oxides, and 33 percent of mercury. In fact,

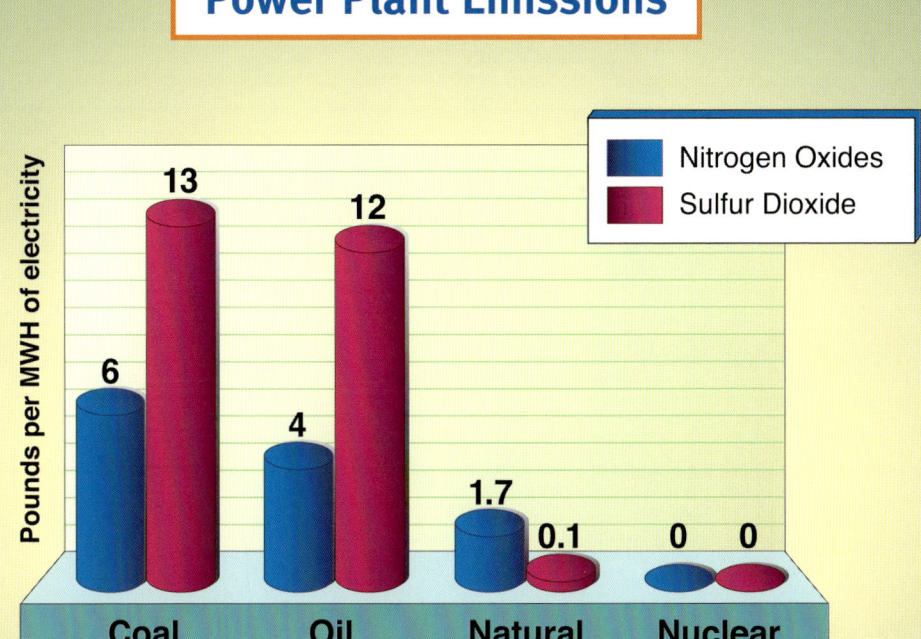

Power plant emissions only, not including small emissions from mining, transportation, and refining or enriching fuel.

Source: U.S. Department of Energy

coal-burning power plants also release 100 times more radioactive material than nuclear power plants do. Fossil fuels contain some uranium. The radioactive elements released by coal-burning plants are not as radioactive as spent nuclear waste. But coal-burning plants release their waste directly into the environment. They do not save it, store it, and shield it, as nuclear plants do with nuclear waste.

A coal-burning power plant in China spews toxic gases, polluting the air.

The Promise of Nuclear Power

Nuclear power plants also produce far less waste than coal-burning plants do. To provide electricity for a city of 1 million people, nuclear plants would have to use about 20 tons (18 metric tons) of uranium. After use, about 52 cubic yards (40 cubic meters) of waste is left, if the fuel is not recycled. If the fuel is recycled, about 9 cubic yards (7 cubic meters) of waste is left. If this waste is buried in a shielded container, ten years of waste would require a space the size of a small home (if the waste is not recycled) or the size of a bedroom (if the waste is recycled).

By contrast, it would take more than 3 million tons (2.7 million metric tons) of coal to produce electricity for a city of 1 million each year. Burning this much coal would produce between 140,000 and 160,000 tons (127,000 and 145,000 metric tons) of ash. About one-third of coal ash in the United States is currently recycled. It gets made into concrete. But the other two-thirds of the ash goes into landfills.

Finally, nuclear supporters point out, the process of mining and burning coal kills many more people every year than accidents at nuclear power plants do. In just two days, more people die in coal-mining accidents than died because of the Chernobyl accident. This even takes into account all the people who died from cancer years after Chernobyl. Chernobyl killed 56 people over the course of twenty years, but coal mining kills 5,000 miners every year. In the United States, 25 out of every 100,000 coal miners can expect to be fatally injured at work. But no workers have ever died of radiation-related accidents at U.S. nuclear power plants. (In the early days of uranium mining, hundreds of miners died from exposure to radiation. But uranium-mining technology has improved, so miners no longer have to go underground. Instead, they pump carbonated water underground, where it dissolves the uranium and brings it back up to the surface.)

Sustainable Nuclear Energy

Some experts say that it should not be necessary to mine any more uranium at all. After nuclear fuel has been used, it still has 95 percent of its energy. If the fuel is reprocessed, much of the remaining energy can still be used. In fact, nuclear waste can be recycled many times. Scientists estimate that enough uranium has already been mined to meet the world's energy needs for the next 500 years.

If scientists discover a way to mine the uranium in ocean water, it is possible that Earth's needs for power could be met for the next 10,000 years. (Extracting uranium from seawater, though, is five

This modern breeder reactor recycles nuclear waste.

to ten times more expensive than mining it on land.) Nuclear energy would still not be renewable, like wind, water, or solar energy. But it would be **sustainable** for vast periods of time, unlike the energy we get from fossil fuels.

How is it possible to recycle used uranium? There are two ways to do it. One way is to recycle it in the reactor itself. Nuclear reactors that do this are called **breeder reactors**, because they make more fuel than they use. France has begun to use breeder reactors. These reactors are very cost-effective. After ten or twenty years of use, one breeder reactor can produce enough fuel to set up another power plant. Breeder reactors use up to 75 percent of the energy in their fuel, while the original generation of nonbreeding reactors uses less than 5 percent.

Unfortunately, older nuclear power plants are not set up to recycle their spent fuel. If they are not converted to newer models, the world's uranium resources could be used up in less than 100 years. On the other hand, spent fuel from older plants can be saved and recycled later. In fact, the world's nuclear reactors have been saving their fuel since they began operating. This is because the countries in which nuclear reactors operate have not authorized any permanent repositories for nuclear waste. (It is not burdensome for nuclear power plants to store nuclear waste on-site because there is so little of it. All the used fuel produced by all the reactors in the United States during the entire history of nuclear power would fill a football field to a depth of about 5 yards, or 4.6 meters.)

Recycling nuclear waste from a plant that is not set up for reprocessing, however, means transporting nuclear waste to a location where it can be reprocessed. Japan, for example, ships its nuclear waste to Europe for reprocessing. Transporting nuclear waste means risking an accident and potential spill. But no such spill has occurred yet.

The Promise of Nuclear Power

Simply holding nuclear waste for decades, though, causes its levels of radioactivity to fall. After 40 years, used fuel has less than one-hundredth of the radioactivity it had when it was first removed from the reactor. Even so, it must still be shielded and stored carefully to protect people and the environment from radiation. But if nuclear fuel is recycled, its radioactivity levels fall even more. When it has been reprocessed so many times that it is finally unusable, it has only about 300 years of high-level

Workers wearing protective suits pump radioactive waste into underground storage tanks at the Hanford nuclear facility in Washington.

The four reactors at a French nuclear power plant can clearly be seen in this aerial view.

radioactivity left. This means that after 300 years, nuclear waste would have no more radioactivity than ordinary uranium.

Nuclear power is not perfectly safe, and a spill or an accident could seriously damage the local environment. Most environmentalists would prefer to rely on renewable energy sources. But a few are beginning to think that nuclear power is the next best option.

Chapter Four

The Future of Nuclear Power

Nuclear power is still controversial. The United States stopped expanding its nuclear industry in the 1970s. Most European countries stopped after the Chernobyl accident in 1986. France was the only European country to continue producing new nuclear power plants, and it did so because it had so few other resources. France has no oil or gas and very little coal.

New Nuclear Power Plants

Twenty years after the Chernobyl accident, France is the most nuclear-dependent country in the world. It relies on 59 nuclear reactors to produce 80 percent of its electricity. France's electric system has drawn attention from other countries because it produces some of the least expensive power in Europe. France's electricity costs consumers 11 cents per kilowatt-hour, while antinuclear countries charge much more. Germany, which is phasing out its nuclear industry, charges 15 cents per kilowatt-hour. Italy, which dismantled its nuclear program after the Chernobyl accident, charges 17 cents. But France must also find a place to store more than 35 million cubic yards (45.8 million cubic meters) of nuclear waste.

A Nuclear Rebirth

Today, France is leading what the industry claims is a nuclear rebirth. Around the world, 25 new reactors are being constructed. Finland is building the first new reactor in Western Europe since 1991. Poland is building a new plant as well. The governments of Great Britain, Italy, and the Netherlands are reconsidering their options. These countries historically have been opposed to nuclear power. Some communities in the United States are also reconsidering nuclear power. One small Alaskan community, Galena, recently voted to build a nuclear reactor.

China and India are expanding their nuclear industries. China, which is increasing its nuclear industry much faster than any other nation, plans to build 32 new nuclear plants. In 2008 Russia will begin operating the world's first commercial floating

A technician studies instruments in the control room of a nuclear power plant in China.

nuclear power plant. Some countries, like Iran, are just beginning to develop nuclear energy programs. In total, 30 countries will produce several hundred more nuclear reactors by 2030. On the other hand, other countries, such as Sweden and Germany, are shutting down their nuclear reactors and plan to build no more.

Global Warming

For many countries, the drive to build more nuclear power plants is a response to global warming. These countries are trying to reduce **carbon dioxide** emissions in order to stop contributing to global warming. Carbon dioxide, or CO_2, is the gas that scientists believe to be responsible for making Earth warmer. Coal-burning power plants contribute a large amount of carbon dioxide emissions. For example, coal-burning power plants in the United States release 2 billion tons (1.8 billion metric tons) of carbon dioxide, the gas that is responsible for global warming, into the air each year. (This amount is equivalent to the exhaust produced by 300 million cars.) They produce 36 percent of U.S. CO_2 emissions, and 10 percent of CO_2 emissions worldwide. Nuclear power plants, on the other hand, do not release any CO_2 into the air.

Scientists estimate that worldwide, 900 tons (816 metric tons) of fossil-fuel emissions are released into the atmosphere every second. Governments hope to reduce those emissions by 60 percent over the next 50 years. But to reduce emissions, they must close some coal-burning power plants. Closing coal-burning power plants is an especially difficult decision, when the demand for electricity is increasing two- or threefold.

If coal-burning power plants are closed, other plants must be built to provide electricity for all the people who need it. Only nuclear and hydroelectric plants can provide electric power without also producing gases that add to global warming. Every 22 tons (20 metric tons) of uranium used in a nuclear

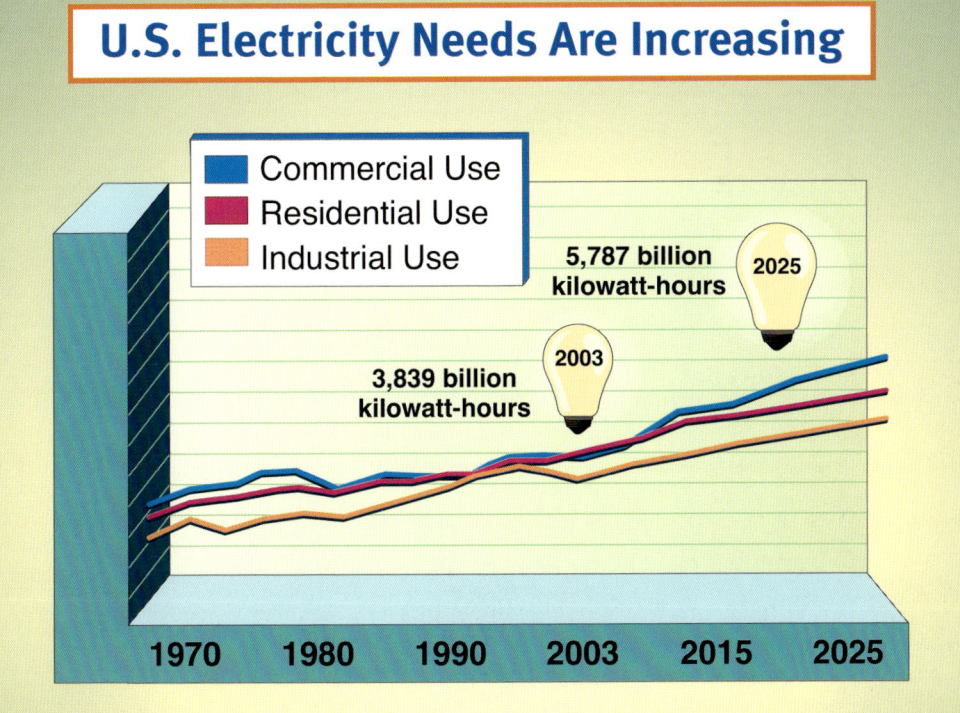

U.S. Electricity Needs Are Increasing

- Commercial Use
- Residential Use
- Industrial Use

3,839 billion kilowatt-hours — 2003

5,787 billion kilowatt-hours — 2025

1970 1980 1990 2003 2015 2025

Source: U.S. Department of Energy

power plant can prevent 1 million tons (.97 million metric tons) of carbon dioxide from being released into the environment by a coal-burning power plant. Every year, just by staying in business, nuclear power plants in the United States prevent the release of about 700 million tons (635 million metric tons) of CO_2. This equals the amount produced by more than 100 million cars.

Global warming has led to greater interest in renewable energy sources such as the electric power generated by these wind turbines.

Increasing World Energy Needs

There is an even more urgent reason why so many countries are reconsidering nuclear energy. As the world's population grows, so does energy consumption. The world's consumption of energy is expected to double by 2050 and to quadruple by 2100. In most countries the demand for electricity is increasing faster than any other energy demand. But the supply of fossil fuels, our primary source of electricity, is running out.

Nobody is sure how long fossil fuels will last. Different fuels will last different amounts of time. Coal will last the longest. At worst, experts predict fossil fuels will last only 50 more years. At best, they say fossil fuels may last several more centuries. Nuclear energy, though, can provide electricity for another thousand years.

Renewable Energy

Renewable forms of energy such as wind power, solar power, and hydroelectric power are better for the environment than fossil fuels or nuclear power. They do not produce air pollution. They also rely on a power supply that can never be used up (wind, moving water, or sunlight).

Currently, though, renewable sources generate less than 10 percent of the world's electricity. Most of this electricity is generated by hydroelectric power plants. In the United States, for instance,

China's Three Gorges Dam (shown here) is the world's largest hydroelectric dam.

solar power, wind power, and power produced by hot springs combined account for less than 1 percent of the nation's electricity. Until these forms of energy are more developed, it does not seem practical to expect them to supply enough electricity to close down any nuclear or coal-burning power plants.

Hydroelectric power plants, where they exist, can produce large amounts of electricity. However, they can only be built in certain places. They require large

The Future of Nuclear Power

rivers with flowing water that can be harnessed. And hydroelectric power plants harm the environment in some ways. They require the building of dams, which can destroy ecosystems. Building dams also forces people to move. For example, 1.2 million people living in more than 500 cities, towns, and villages had to move when China built its Three Gorges Dam. Their former homes were flooded by the deepwater reservoir that the dam formed.

People cannot yet rely on renewable energy to provide much electricity. At the same time, the supply of fossil fuels is running out. Nuclear energy may be the only energy source left that can provide cheap electricity to massive numbers of people.

The decision to use nuclear power plants to generate electricity is not one that most countries can make easily. Decision makers must consider the costs of different methods of generating power. They need to think about the possible effects on the environment. They need to think about safety. They also need to consider the opinions of the people who live in the area. As the world's population increases and the demand for electricity goes up, though, it is likely that more and more countries will come to rely on nuclear power plants.

Glossary

breeder reactors: Reactors that make more fuel than they use, by recycling spent fuel.

carbon dioxide (CO_2): A gas that contributes to global warming by causing a greenhouse effect in Earth's atmosphere. It lets heat from the Sun enter Earth's atmosphere but blocks much of it from being reflected back out into space.

chain reaction: The process by which a fissioning atom of uranium starts splitting other atoms of uranium by sending off two or three neutrons to hit their nuclei.

fission: Splitting the nucleus of an atom.

nuclear forces: The forces that bind the nucleus of an atom together and prevent nuclear particles from escaping the atom.

nuclear power: Energy that is generated by splitting the nucleus of an atom.

nuclear waste: Spent nuclear fuel.

nucleus: The center of an atom.

radiation: Energy that travels in particles or waves. Examples include sunlight, radio waves, microwaves, and X-rays. Radioactivity is also a kind of radiation.

radioactive: Giving off particles from an atom's nucleus.

sustainable: Able to be maintained for a long period of time without running out.

uranium: An element that is used as fuel for nuclear power reactors.

For Further Exploration

Books

Burgan, Michael, et al. *Nuclear Energy.* Discovery Channel School Science series. Milwaukee: Gareth Stevens, 2002. Covers the history of nuclear energy, its benefits and risks, and possible uses for it in the future.

Juettner, Bonnie. *Energy.* San Diego: Kidhaven, 2005. Part of KidHaven's Our Environment series. Covers world energy use and trends in energy supply and demand.

Kidd, J.S., and Renee Kidd. *Nuclear Power: The Study of Quarks and Sparks.* New York: Facts On File, 2006. Covers other potential uses for nuclear energy, such as medical imaging and making new products.

Richardson, Hazel. *How to Split the Atom.* London: Franklin Watts, 2001. Explains the difference between atoms, molecules, elements, and compounds. Also covers the parts of an atom and the basics of how atoms are split.

For Further Exploration

Web Sites

"Energy." Fact Monster Science, from Information Please. (http://www.factmonster.com/ipka/A0909524.html). Provides general information on world energy use, including a breakdown of the world's biggest energy suppliers and consumers.

Energy Information Administration Energy Kids Page (www.eia.doe.gov/kids/energyfacts/sources/non-renewable/nuclear.html). The Web site of the Energy Information Administration explains how nuclear energy works and shows diagrams of nuclear reactors. Links lead to information about other forms of energy.

Energy Quest (www.energyquest.ca.gov/index.html). The Web site of the California Energy Commission includes links to information about all kinds of energy. It also has science projects, including a project that uses dominoes to explain how a nuclear chain reaction can take place.

"The Greenhouse Effect." Global Warming Kids Site. (http://www.epa.gov/globalwarming/kids/greenhouse.html) This Web site is maintained by the U.S. Environmental Protection Agency. It explains how global warming works and what the greenhouse effect is.

Index

accidents, 18–23, 28
aircraft carriers, 10
air pollution, 25, 39
ash, 27
atoms, 4–7

breeder reactors, 29–30

carbon dioxide (CO_2) emissions, 36–38
carbon nucleus, 7
chain reactions, 20
Chernobyl accident, 18–20, 28
China, 34, 41
coal
  deaths from mining accidents, 27–28
  energy from, 7
  power plants burning, 8, 25–27, 36

dams, 41
deaths
from coal mining accidents, 27–28
from nuclear accidents, 19, 23, 28

ecosystems, 41
electricity
  costs in Europe, 34
  demand, 37
  sources, 8–10, 25, 39–40
energy
  consumption in future, 39
  from fission, 7
  renewable, 39–41
  sustainable, 29
environment, 24–25, 32, 41
Europe, 34
  see also specific countries

Finland, 34
fission, 7–8
food chains, 16
fossil fuels
  coal-burning power plants, 8, 25–27, 36
  coal-mining accident deaths, 27–28
  emissions, 36–38
  energy from coal, 7
  supply, 33, 39
France
  breeder reactors, 29–30
  electricity costs, 34
  reliance on nuclear power, 10, 33–34

Galena, Alaska, 34
Germany
  electricity costs, 34
  nuclear power plant closures, 13, 36
global warming, 36–38
Great Britain, 22, 34

heat, 14
Hoover Dam, 8
hydroelectric power plants, 8, 37, 40–41

India, 34
Iran, 36
Italy, 13, 34

Japan, 17, 23, 30

landfills, 27
Lithuania, 10

mass, 5

Index

mercury, 25
microwaves, 14
Mihama (Japan), 23
mining, 27–28

Netherlands, 34
neutrons, 7
nitrous oxides, 25
nuclear forces, 5–7, 13–14
nuclear-powered vehicles, 10
nuclear power plants
  accidents, 18–23, 28
  building new, 33–34, 36
  closing, 13, 36
  electricity from, 8, 9
  number worldwide, 9–10
  recycling fuel and, 29–30
  uranium needs, 27
  see also nuclear waste
nuclear waste
  from France, 34
  radioactivity, 15–16, 27
  reprocessing, 17
  storing, 16–18, 30
nuclei
  described, 4–5
  nuclear forces and, 5–7, 13–14
  splitting, 7–8
nucleons
  in carbon, 7
  nucleus size and, 6
  in U-235, 7

oceans, 28
Ohio, 21

pollution, 25, 39

radiation, 14
radioactivity, 13–14
  from Chernobyl accident, 18–19
  from coal-burning power plants, 26
  leaks, 22, 23
  lowering levels, 31–32
  of uranium, 14–16
radio waves, 14
recycling, 17
  see also reprocessing nuclear waste
rems, 16

renewable energy, 9, 37, 39–41
reprocessing nuclear waste
  accident in Britain, 22
  in Europe, 30
  by Japan, 17
  United States and, 17–18
  uranium needs and, 28
Russia, 10, 34, 36

submarines, 10
sulfur dioxide, 25
sunlight, 14
sustainable energy, 29
Sweden, 36

Three Gorges Dam, 41
Tokaimura (Japan), 23
transportation of nuclear waste, 17–18, 30

Ukraine, 18–20, 28
United States
  building nuclear power plants, 13, 34
  carbon dioxide emissions, 36, 38
  deaths from coal mining accidents, 28
  electricity from renewable energy sources, 39–40
  energy from nuclear power, 10
  nuclear-powered ships, 10
  nuclear power plant accidents, 21, 22
  nuclear waste and, 17–18, 30
uranium-235 (U-235)
  energy from, 7–8
  needs of large ships, 10
  needs of nuclear power plants, 27, 28
  nucleus, 7
  radioactivity, 14–16, 32

vehicles, nuclear-powered, 10
volume, 5

waste. *See* nuclear waste

X-rays, 14

Yucca Mountain, Nevada, 18

Zorita (Spain), 21

About the Author

Bonnie Juettner is a writer and editor of children's reference books and educational videos. Originally from McGrath, Alaska, she currently lives in Kenosha, Wisconsin. This is her tenth book.